SECRETS OF THE ANIMAL WORLD

DOLPHINS
Animals with Sonar

by Andreu Llamas
Illustrated by Gabriel Casadevall and Ali Garousi

Gareth Stevens Publishing
MILWAUKEE

For a free color catalog describing Gareth Stevens' list of high-quality books, call 1-800-542-2595 (USA) or 1-800-461-9120 (Canada). Gareth Stevens' Fax: (414) 225-0377.

The editor would like to extend special thanks to Jan W. Rafert, Curator of Primates and Small Mammals, Milwaukee County Zoo, Milwaukee, Wisconsin, for his kind and professional help with the information in this book.

Library of Congress Cataloging-in-Publication Data

Llamas, Andreu.
    [Delfin. English]
    Dolphins: animals with sonar / by Andreu Llamas; illustrated by Gabriel Casadevall and Ali Garousi.
        p.   cm. — (Secrets of the animal world)
    Includes bibliographical references (p.   ) and index.
    Summary: Provides detailed descriptions of the physical characteristics and behavior of dolphins.
    ISBN 0-8368-1395-2 (lib. bdg.)
    1. Dolphins—Juvenile literature.   [1. Dolphins.]   I. Casadevall, Gabriel, ill.   II. Garousi, Ali, ill.   III. Title.   IV. Series.
    QL737.C432L5813   1996
    599.5'3—dc20   95-45801

This North American edition first published in 1996 by
Gareth Stevens Publishing
1555 North RiverCenter Drive, Suite 201
Milwaukee, Wisconsin 53212 USA

This U.S. edition © 1996 by Gareth Stevens, Inc. Created with original © 1993 Ediciones Este, S.A., Barcelona, Spain. Additional end matter © 1996 by Gareth Stevens, Inc.

Series editor: Patricia Lantier-Sampon
Editorial assistants: Diane Laska, Rita Reitci, Derek Smith.

Printed in the United States of America

1 2 3 4 5 6 7 8 9 99 98 97 96

CONTENTS

THE DOLPHIN'S WORLD

Watery habitat

More than thirty different species of dolphins live in the world's seas and oceans, as well as the great rivers of Asia and South America. Even though they live in water, dolphins are mammals; they have to come to the surface regularly to breathe air into their lungs.

Dolphins are well adapted to sea life. They can dive deeper than 900 feet (275 m) and swim as fast as 25 miles (40 km) an hour.

Dolphins love to perform incredible acrobatics. In the photograph above, a dolphin makes a spectacular leap.

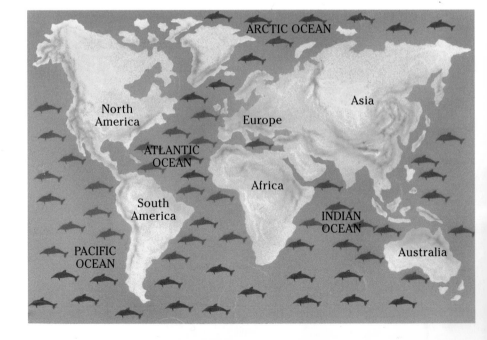

Dolphins live in cold, polar waters, as well as in warm, tropical waters.

ARCTIC OCEAN

North America

Asia

Europe

ATLANTIC OCEAN

Africa

South America

INDIAN OCEAN

PACIFIC OCEAN

Australia

A complex brain

The dolphin is an intelligent animal. It communicates with other dolphins, using sounds. It can learn to do complex tasks, solve simple problems, and even mimic some human words. One indication of mental ability is the number of folds in the cortex, that part of the brain involved with learning and thinking. Some dolphins have 50 percent more folds in their cortex than a human brain. But it is difficult to study the dolphin's intelligence because many of its brain functions involve its guidance system.

Some dolphin brains have 50 percent more folds (circumvolutions) than the brains of humans.

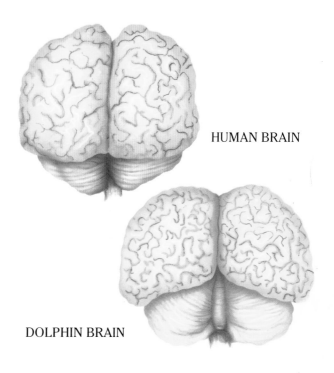

HUMAN BRAIN

DOLPHIN BRAIN

Dolphins can untie the knots of fishermen's nets.

Many kinds of dolphins

Dolphins are mammals that have undergone many physical changes to adapt to life in the water. These animals belong to the family Delphinidae, which includes at least thirty-one species, some of which are totally different from others. Whales, for example, belong to the same family as the dolphin.

Dolphins are streamlined in shape, most with a pointed beak at the end of the animal's head. They are found both in the high seas and in coastal waters. They usually swim in groups that can number hundreds and even thousands of dolphins.

Some dolphins live in rivers. The river dolphins belong to the family Platanistidae instead of the family Delphinidae. These pictures show how different species of dolphins vary in shape and color.

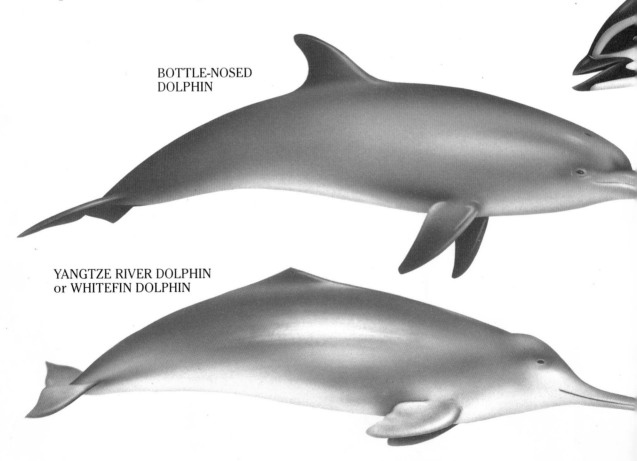

BOTTLE-NOSED DOLPHIN

YANGTZE RIVER DOLPHIN or WHITEFIN DOLPHIN

COMMON DOLPHIN

FRASER'S DOLPHIN

HOURGLASS DOLPHIN

SPOTTED DOLPHIN

7

INSIDE THE DOLPHIN

Dolphins belong to the order Cetacea and the suborder Odontoceti. All dolphins have a hydrodynamic body; their streamlined shape enables them to swim through water with little friction. They propel themselves with their tail fin, moving it up and down to swim forward. Their pectoral fins, or flippers, increase the animals' stability. Here you can see the internal characteristics of a bottle-nosed dolphin.

RIBS
The dolphin's ribs are delicate. They are not firmly connected to any other part of the dolphin's anatomy.

KIDNEYS

INTESTINE

TESTICLES

CAUDAL, or TAIL FIN
This fin is positioned sideways, but the animal moves it up and down to drive ahead. The dolphin can reach high speeds and jump great heights because of this powerful fin.

ANUS

PENIS   STOMACH

SKIN
The skin is soft and hairless. This helps the dolphin swim faster, since water runs more smoothly over its body. Its skin must always be wet, even when it is moved from one aquarium to another.

BLUBBER
A layer of fat and oil that lies in a thick coat under the skin. The blubber is several inches (cm) thick, which enables the animal to keep warm in the water.

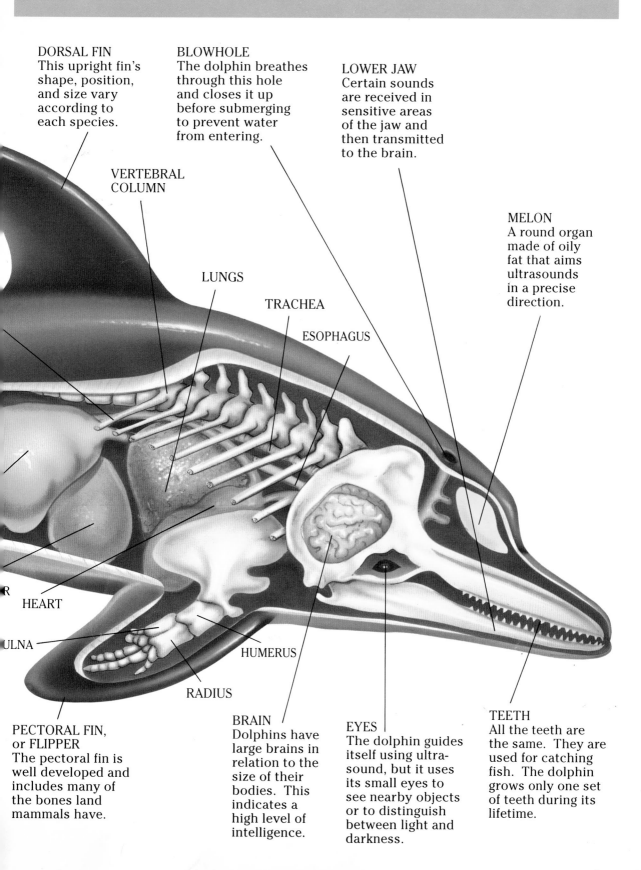

DORSAL FIN
This upright fin's shape, position, and size vary according to each species.

BLOWHOLE
The dolphin breathes through this hole and closes it up before submerging to prevent water from entering.

LOWER JAW
Certain sounds are received in sensitive areas of the jaw and then transmitted to the brain.

VERTEBRAL COLUMN

MELON
A round organ made of oily fat that aims ultrasounds in a precise direction.

LUNGS

TRACHEA

ESOPHAGUS

HEART

ULNA

HUMERUS

RADIUS

PECTORAL FIN, or FLIPPER
The pectoral fin is well developed and includes many of the bones land mammals have.

BRAIN
Dolphins have large brains in relation to the size of their bodies. This indicates a high level of intelligence.

EYES
The dolphin guides itself using ultrasound, but it uses its small eyes to see nearby objects or to distinguish between light and darkness.

TEETH
All the teeth are the same. They are used for catching fish. The dolphin grows only one set of teeth during its lifetime.

DOLPHIN SONAR

Light and sound under water

Light diffuses differently in water than in air. Light is quickly absorbed under water. Even in clear water, it is very difficult to see farther away than 30 to 65 feet (10 to 20 m). For marine animals, this can create a serious problem in identifying prey and enemies from a distance. Dolphins have developed a solution to this problem, using sounds. Water is eight hundred times denser than air, so sound travels five times faster in water than in air.

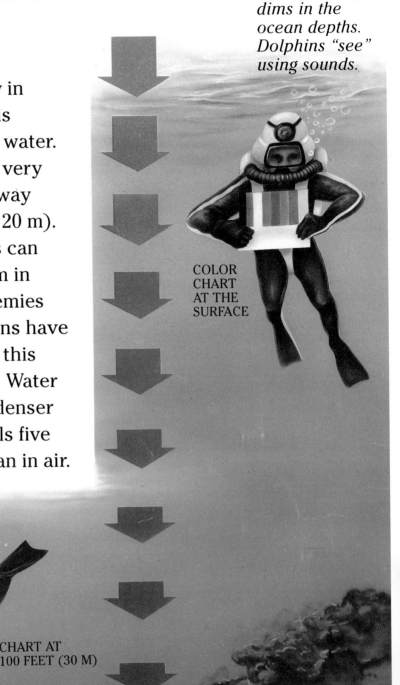

This color chart shows how light dims in the ocean depths. Dolphins "see" using sounds.

COLOR CHART AT THE SURFACE

CHART AT 100 FEET (30 M)

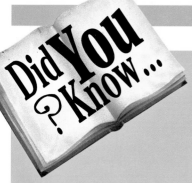
that dolphins have a poor sense of smell?

Through evolution, dolphins have gradually lost their sense of smell. Their nostrils shifted position, and their nasal ducts began to work differently. The dolphin would drown if water got into its lungs. To avoid this danger, the animal has strong muscles that close the blowhole and nasal passages when it submerges. The only time the blowhole opens is when the dolphin comes to the surface for air.

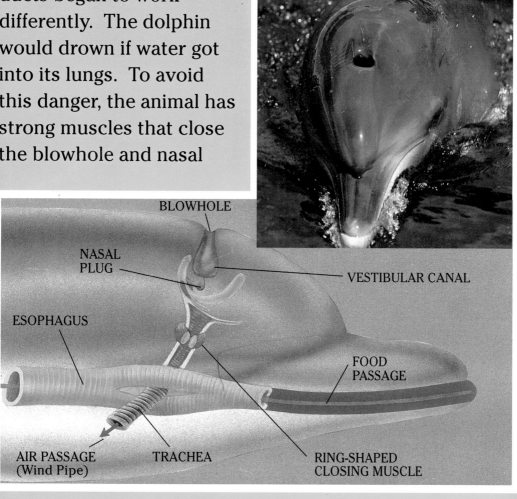

BLOWHOLE

NASAL
PLUG

VESTIBULAR CANAL

ESOPHAGUS

FOOD
PASSAGE

AIR PASSAGE
(Wind Pipe)

TRACHEA

RING-SHAPED
CLOSING MUSCLE

Echolocation

Dolphins use sounds to obtain information about their surroundings. This ability is called echolocation. The dolphin makes two types of sounds: first, it whistles to communicate and "speak" with other dolphins; second, it makes a clicking noise to guide itself.

When dolphins swim in the sea, and there is nothing nearby, they produce a constant, low-frequency signal. This signal tells the position of the coast, the type of seabed, depth, and other information.

When a dolphin receives a new echo, it tries to obtain more information: How far away is it?

The dolphin's echolocation is accurate for detecting objects.

Which direction is it headed? Is it a shark? The dolphin makes a series of different clicks (each time with a higher frequency) as it moves closer. The resulting echoes give the dolphin more precise information about the object. The clicks become more frequent and sound like a continuous repetition.

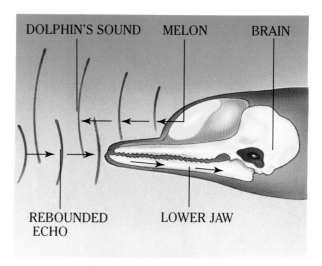

THE DOLPHIN'S LANGUAGE

Dolphin whistles

The dolphin's brain is as large as or even larger than a human's. Some scientists believe the dolphins can produce superior thought processes. They are able to make a wide variety of different sounds, and many in captivity imitate the whistles of trainers as though they want to communicate. Experiments have been carried out in which two dolphins in different aquariums "spoke" to each other over a kind of telephone. Both dolphins whistled and made other sounds, but they stopped when the telephone was disconnected and only

One dolphin communicates over a "telephone" with another in a separate aquarium.

Dolphins love to stick their heads out of the water to communicate and see what is happening.

produced their usual identification whistles. It is difficult for scientists to decipher the meaning of these whistles because humans cannot hear sounds above 14,000 vibrations of air per second. Dolphins, however, can easily produce sounds of up to 300,000 vibrations per second.

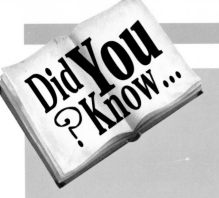

that there are blind dolphins?

More than a dozen species of freshwater dolphins live in rivers. One species is the Ganges River dolphin, which is almost blind. Its small eyes can only distinguish between light and dark. It moves around using only echolocation. Sight would be of little use anyway in the muddy rivers where the dolphin lives. The Ganges River dolphin usually swims on one side in order to trail the edge of its flipper along the bottom of the river.

16

Better than the Navy

When the U.S. Navy began to develop the first sonar devices, workers learned that dolphins used sounds to explore. The dolphin's echolocation is much better than systems used on aircraft carriers or submarines because humans use more limited frequencies than dolphins. The dolphin produces sound from air contained in its respiratory passages, and then the melon aims these sounds in the correct direction. If the sounds rebound from an object, they are picked up by the lower jaw and transmitted to the middle ear and then the brain, which identifies them.

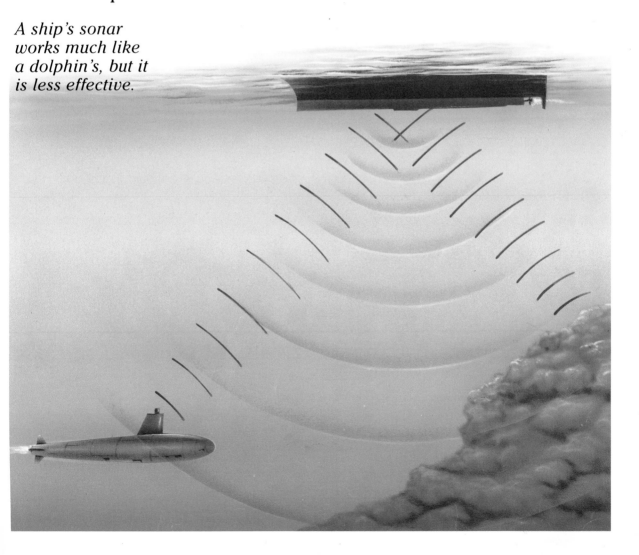

A ship's sonar works much like a dolphin's, but it is less effective.

ANCESTORS OF THE DOLPHINS

The first dolphins

Dolphins have existed for over twelve million years. But the dolphin's ancestors, the Archaeoceti, inhabited the seas more than forty million years ago. These primitive dolphins had trouble adapting to sea life because other dangerous animals, such as sharks, had several million years head start to perfect their senses of smell and hearing. Evolution gave the dolphins an effective, sonarlike system and a streamlined body that allowed them to swim fast.

The Archaeoceti had fewer but larger teeth than today's dolphins.

Modern dolphins can have over 200 teeth.

The Archaeoceti were primitive dolphins that lived in the sea forty million years ago.

Giving birth under water

As they evolved, dolphins learned to give birth under water without drowning the offspring. After a gestation period lasting from nine to eighteen months, the offspring is born tail first. When the newborn is free of its mother, one or two other dolphins help it up to the surface so it does not drown. The lactation period normally lasts over a year, and the young dolphin has to nurse under water. It stays near the surface so it can go up to breathe.

Adult dolphins take turns keeping the newborn afloat on the surface.

The shape of the dolphin's body enables it to give birth to its young tail first.

THE LIFE OF THE DOLPHIN

Sharks and dolphins: enemies forever

Dolphins have very few enemies in the sea. Only sharks and whales hunt them, and these predators tend to pursue sick or young dolphins. Sharks often follow dolphin pods in the hope of catching one of the young or sick stragglers. When a dolphin is attacked, it thrusts its beak into the shark's gills or stomach, the most vulnerable parts of the creature's body. Dolphins also work together in times of danger.

Dolphins swim in groups, or pods, that may contain many individuals.

A dolphin defends itself against sharks by striking with its beak.

that dolphins know how to surf?

Dolphins like to swim alongside boats. A sailing ship or boat moving in the water creates waves. Dolphins will often approach a boat, not in search of food, but to have some fun surfing on the waves produced by the boat's movement. The dolphins ride on the back of the waves and let gravity push them forward, like surfers at the beach.

Humans and dolphins

As early as the year 109, a true story had been written about a friendship between a child and a dolphin named Simo. There are also many stories of dolphins saving the lives of drowning humans. Many dolphins try to communicate with people, and some species enjoy spending the summer alongside bathers. Dolphins often let swimmers touch them.

Contact between dolphins and people is not always positive, however. One of the

There are many documented cases of dolphins coming to the rescue of drowning humans. This may relate to the dolphins' habit of keeping their young afloat.

worst dangers for the dolphin is the tuna fishing industry, which causes the deaths of hundreds of thousands of dolphins that get trapped in the fishing nets. But in some tropical countries, fishermen train the dolphins to help drive fish into their nets. The fishermen then share their catch with the dolphins.

In Australia's Shark's Bay, dolphins are a major tourist attraction. The dolphins approach the beach and let people stroke and feed them. Over forty thousand people from around the world visit the dolphins each year.

Dolphins can do all sorts of incredible acrobatics.

APPENDIX TO

SECRETS
OF THE
ANIMAL WORLD

DOLPHINS
Animals with Sonar

DOLPHIN SECRETS

▼ **A record number of teeth.** Some dolphins have up to 260 teeth, which is a record among mammals.

▼ **Sharklike teeth.** Several primitive dolphins that lived about 25 million years ago had teeth similar to sharks.

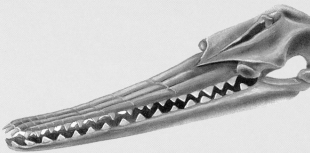

▼ **Dolphins that lose their sonar.** Dolphins in captivity become deafened by their own echo-location sounds. After living in aquariums for many years, they no longer use their sonar system.

Very little sleep. Dolphins sleep only two to three hours a day, but they are sometimes so tired they are hit by boats while floating on the surface.

Eating at night. Some dolphins spend daytime near the coast, and at night they move into deeper waters to eat fish.

▶ Dolphin dictionary.
Russian scientists are producing a "dolphin dictionary," but they still cannot understand what dolphins are saying.

"Guard-dog" dolphins.
Scientists train dolphins to watch for sharks. The dolphin receives a signal, tracks the shark, and attacks it. Scientists hope they will soon be able to use dolphins to protect divers from sharks.

1. Where do dolphins live?
a) In the sea.
b) In rivers.
c) Some species live in the sea, while others live in rivers.

2. What is a blowhole?
a) A floating organ.
b) A breathing hole.
c) A greasy tissue near the tail.

3. The dolphin can swim at a speed of:
a) 12 miles (20 km) an hour.
b) 10 miles (16 km) an hour.
c) 25 miles (40 km) an hour.

4. Dolphins are:
a) fishes.
b) mammals.
c) amphibians.

5. Sound under water travels:
a) twice as slow as in the air.
b) 30 times faster than in the air.
c) 5 times faster than in the air.

6. How many species of dolphins are there?
a) At least 31.
b) At least 90.
c) At least 150.

The answers to DOLPHIN SECRETS questions are on page 32.

GLOSSARY

blowhole: a small hole located on top of the dolphin's head that the dolphin uses to breathe. By swimming up to the surface and raising the blowhole above the water, the dolphin can breathe air without getting water into its lungs. Strong muscles keep the blowhole closed while the dolphin is below the water.

Cetacea: the scientific order to which all dolphins belong. This order also includes whales and porpoises.

circumvolutions (brain folds): Brain tissue forms many crevices called folds. These are related to how information is received, stored, and recalled. The more folds, the more complex the brain and its functions. In dolphins, the brain is highly developed and contains many folds.

Delphinidae: the scientific family to which most dolphins belong. The other family to which dolphins belong, called Platanistidae, includes mostly river and inland water dwelling species. The Delphinidae family also includes some whales and porpoises. While classifying certain species of dolphins, whales, and porpoises can be difficult because they share many features, all Delphinidae have teeth in the upper and lower jaws.

dorsal fin: a fin that rises from the back of most dolphins. Similar to the dorsal fin of a shark, this fin can be seen above the water when a dolphin swims just below the surface, and it helps the dolphin keep its balance in the water. However, not all dolphins have such a noticeable dorsal fin. Some species in the Platanistidae family have very small dorsal fins, and on some it is little more than a ridge on the back.

echolocation: the dolphin's navigation system, which works like the sonar of humans. Dolphins send out signals, called ultrasounds, that bounce, or echo, off its surroundings. These ultrasounds then return to the dolphin to give it a clear sound-picture of its location and the objects in the area.

esophagus: the tube through which food gets from the mouth to the stomach.

evolution: the process of changing or developing gradually from one form to another. Over time, all living things evolve to survive in their changing environments or they become extinct.

gestation: the period of time in the reproductive cycle from conception to birth.

humerus: the bone, found in the flipper, that connects the shoulder to the ulna and radius.

hydrodynamic: the shape an object has that allows it to move easily through water. Dolphin bodies are hydro-dynamic; they have smooth and tight skin on a body that is tapered at both ends. This shape helps reduce resistance in moving through water as the dolphin swims.

lactation: the process of secreting milk to feed offspring.

melon: a mysterious organ found in all animals of the dolphin suborder Odontoceti. The melon is a bump located in the front of the head above the upper jaw. While the exact function of this organ puzzles scientists, it has something to do with sound transmission and the dolphin's navigational system. Scientists believe the sonarlike sounds that dolphins send out to gain information about their surroundings originate here. The melon is filled with melon oil, which is a good sound transmitter.

Odontoceti: the scientific suborder to which all dolphins belong. The animals in this group have teeth. Some whales and all porpoises also belong to this group.

pectoral fins: flippers that extend from the side of the body and help steer the dolphin.

Platanistidae: the scientific family to which only a few dolphins belong. The five species of dolphins that belong to this family are river-dwellers.

radius: a bone in the flipper located just in front of the ulna and just above the dolphin's "finger" bones.

testicles: male reproductive organs where sperm is produced.

trachea: the main breathing tube that carries air into the lungs.

ulna: a bone in the flipper behind the radius and above the dolphin's "finger" bones.

ultrasounds: sound waves of a very high frequency. Dolphins produce ultrasounds to navigate and sense their surroundings. These sound waves echo off objects in the water and then return to the dolphin to give it a sound-picture of its environment.

ACTIVITIES

◆ Dolphins can be trained to do complex tasks. They can even teach themselves to perform complex movements simply by watching humans and other animals. Visit a local aquarium or one of the aquariums listed in this book and observe the dolphin's activities firsthand. Bring a notebook and record the similarities between dolphin activity and humans and other animals, such as dogs, lions, and other creatures that can be trained. Do you think dolphins are highly intelligent and aware of what their actions mean, or are they merely mimicking what they see?

◆ Few animals occur in myth and legend as frequently as the dolphins. Visit the library and research some of the fantastic stories that surround dolphins. Some people believe dolphins are connected to the lost city of Atlantis. Others believe communing with dolphins has spiritual and healing effects. There are even stories of dolphins saving drowning people at sea or leading ships to safety. After you find out more about these stories, do you believe any of them? Can any be explained scientifically, or are dolphins magical creatures?

MORE BOOKS TO READ

A Charm of Dolphins. Howard Hall (Blake Publishing)
Dolphin. Sue Houghton (Troll Associates)
Dolphin Adventure: A True Story. Wayne Grover (Morrow)
Dolphin Magic for Kids. Patricia Corrigan (Gareth Stevens)
Dolphins. Norman S. Barrett (Watts)
Dolphins. (Raintree Steck-Vaughn)
Dolphins and Porpoises. Dorothy H. Patent (Holiday)
Nine True Dolphin Stories. Margaret Davidson (Scholastic)
The Sea World Book of Dolphins. Stephen Leatherwood and
    Randall Reeves (Harcourt Brace)
Whales and Dolphins. Francene Sabin (Troll Associates)
Whales and Dolphins. Strachan (Trafalgar)
Whales, Dolphins and Porpoises. Mark Carwardine (Dorling Kindersley)

VIDEOS

Dolphin Adventure. (Live Home Video/ Vestron Video/ Sports on Video)
The Dolphin Touch. (Public Media Video/ Wishing Well Distributing)
Dolphins. (National Geographic Society)
Dolphins: Our Friends from the Sea. (AIMS Media)
Dolphins, Whales, and Us. (Bennett Marine Video)

PLACES TO VISIT

**Sea World on the
    Gold Coast**
Sea World Drive Spit
Surfers Paradise
Queensland, Australia
4217

Sea World
1720 South Shores Road
San Diego, CA 92109

John G. Shedd Aquarium
1200 South Lake Shore
    Drive
Chicago, IL 60605

Vancouver Aquarium
In Stanley Park
Vancouver, British
    Columbia V6B 3X8

**Mystic Marinelife
    Aquarium**
55 Coogan Boulevard
Mystic, CT 06355

Marineland
Marine Parade
Napier, New Zealand

INDEX

**Answers to
DOLPHIN SECRETS
questions:**
1. c
2. b
3. c
4. b
5. c
6. a